I0759887

MESSI'S

MAGIC

How Lionel Messi Became the G.O.A.T.

by Caroline L. Perry
illustrated by Luciano Lozano

Scholastic Press / New York

Lionel "Leo" Messi

was born in Rosario, Argentina,

a city garnished with green

and wrapped by the Paraná River.

In Rosario, factories hummed,

bicycles clattered,

and tango dancers twirled.

But everything stopped for soccer.

10
MARADONA
10

Baby Leo's parents didn't have much money,

but the family home was loving,

noisy, and soccer obsessed.

Before he could even walk, Leo watched his older brothers,

Rodrigo and Matías, kick and block, dribble and dart,

and send balls flying into the back of the net.

Each time they scored, **Leo roared!**

And as soon as he could stand,

Leo joined in.

Toddle. Tap!

Wobble. Whack!

Stagger. Send!

Sprint. **SHOOT!**

When Leo was only four, his grandma Celia took him to the neighborhood soccer club.

"He's too young," Grandoli's coach said. "He'll get hurt!"

But Grandoli's team was missing a player, and Grandma Celia insisted that Leo take his place.

"Let him play!" she demanded.

On the field, Leo made contact.

GOAAAAALLLLLLL!

He tackled and shot.

GOAAAAALLLLLLL!

The tiniest player scored twice!

Just two years later, Leo tried out for a bigger club.

At Newell's Old Boys, the stakes were higher.

Leo dribbled around defenders.

He flicked his left foot.

GOAAAAALLLLLL!!!!

Onlookers cheered.

Grandma Celia roared!

NOB

At school, Leo was the smallest in his class.

He was timid,

and his words sometimes got stuck.

Soccer was Leo's passion.

During recess and lunch,

Leo spoke with his feet.

With a ball, Leo made magic.

The shy boy shone.

Leo's soccer coach cooked up a recipe to multiply his magic.

His star player was a picky eater, but he loved treats.

"For every goal you score, I'll give you a chocolate cookie!" the coach said.

Leo's shots got even sweeter.

He jumped around opponents,

leaving defenders in the dust.

His brothers called him

"La Pulguita" — the little flea.

He left his rivals hopping mad!

In six seasons, Leo scored almost 500 goals and scarfed down a lot of cookies! He was the club champion. The little flea had the world at his nimble feet.

But one sunless day, sadness struck.

His beloved grandma Celia died.

Leo's heart felt heavy.

And doctors worried about Leo's health, too. He wasn't growing like his teammates.

Tests were ordered. Leo was examined. Measured. Poked and pricked.

When the results came in, they showed that Leo had a problem with the part of his body that makes bones and muscles develop.

He needed daily injections, but the treatment was very expensive and his family couldn't afford it.

Without the medicine,

Leo wouldn't grow.

He could never be

a professional player.

Leo's parents worked even harder,

but Leo didn't like to see them struggle.

He did the only thing he could:

He practiced, day and night,

to make his skills even stronger.

Leo was small,

but he had skyscraping dreams.

Maradona
10

When Leo was thirteen, he was offered a trial with FC Barcelona,

one of Europe's top soccer clubs!

Leo was usually calm under pressure,

but in Spain, his heart fluttered.

His tummy twisted.

Would his feet know what to do?

FCB

On the field, Leo dribbled, danced, and dazzled.

Bounce. **Block!**

Dash. **Drive!**

Charge. **Carry!**

Sprint. **SHOOT!**

SCORE!

Barcelona's boss was bewitched.

"We have to sign this kid right now," he said.

He wrote a contract on a paper napkin!

The club agreed to pay for Leo's medical treatment

and to nurture his talent.

The little flea was flying!

But at La Masia soccer academy, Leo struggled.

Training schedules were intense.

He had to stick needles into his legs every night

to deliver the medicine his body needed.

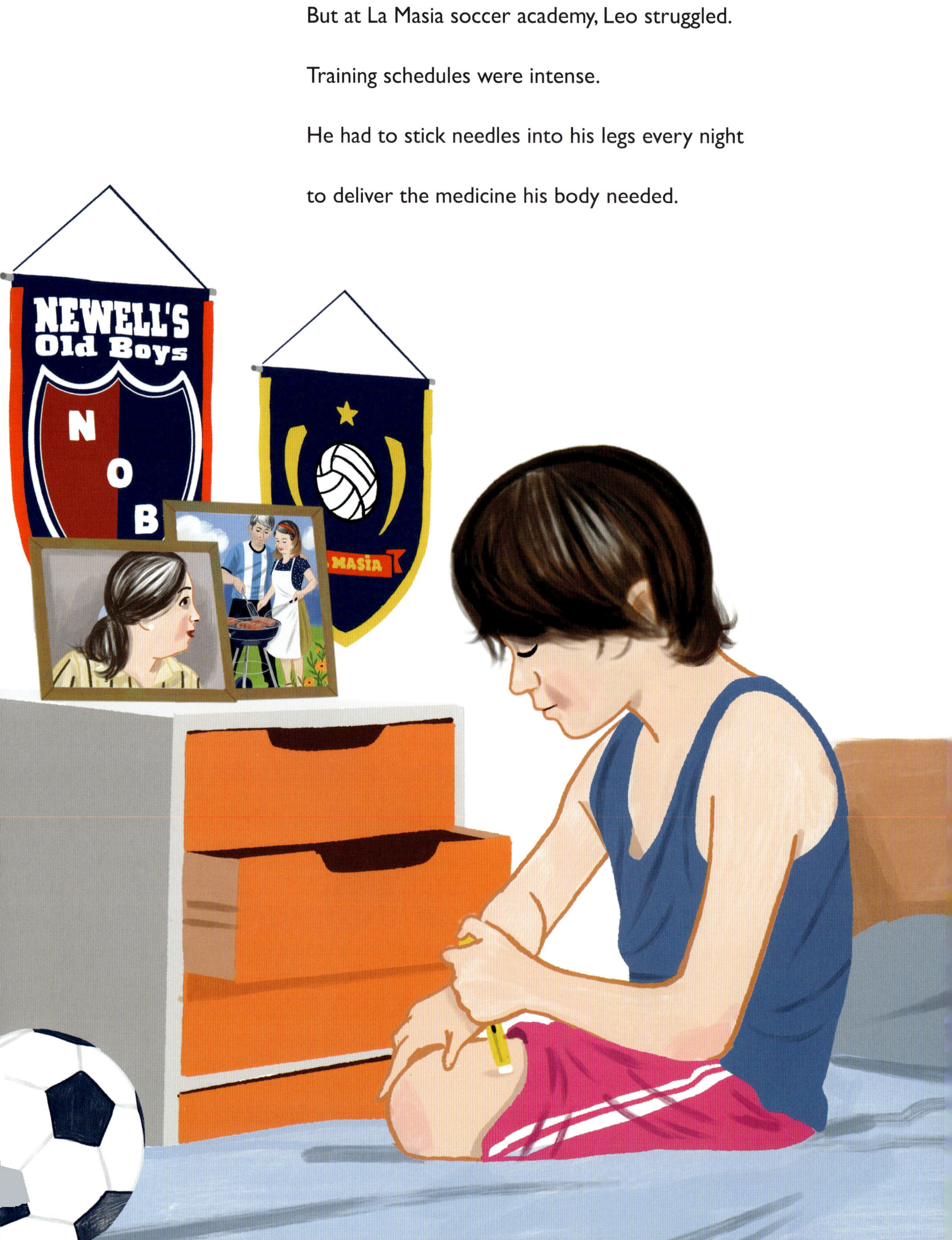

And making friends wasn't easy.

Leo often cried himself to sleep

and wished himself back to his loving,

noisy, soccer-obsessed home.

He never imagined his dream would feel so lonely.

Some days, sadness wrapped Leo like a heavy blanket.

But only the best youth players became stars.

He couldn't miss this shot.

On game day, Leo was laser-focused.

He pushed worries from his mind.

Now it was just him and the ball,

his oldest friend in the world.

Leo dashed around defenders.

GOAAAAALLLLLLLLL!!!!

He set up stunning assists.

GOAAAAALLLLLLLLL!!!!

He glided past goalies.

GOAAAAALLLLLLLLL!!!!

Leo wowed every crowd.

GOAAAAALLLLLLLLL!!!!

At just seventeen, Leo achieved his dream.

He was promoted to FC Barcelona's first team!

All eyes were on him,

the new kid on the field.

His heart fluttered.

His tummy twisted.

But his feet knew what to do.

When Leo scored,

90,000 fans roared!

Not every game was a success.

Sometimes, the final score stung.

But Leo couldn't let it keep him down.

Once again, he practiced,

day and night,

to make his skills even stronger.

In game after game,

each time Leo's ball smashed into the back of the net,

he pointed two fingers up to the sky,

dedicating the goals to Grandma Celia.

The shy, soccer-obsessed kid had made it.

And he knew he'd made her proud.

At his clubs FC Barcelona, Paris Saint-Germain, and Inter Miami,

and for his country, Argentina,

the little flea

became a goal-scoring sensation,

winning the most professional awards of any player.

When he scores,

millions of Messi fans roar!

Leo's home is still loving,

noisy,

and soccer obsessed.

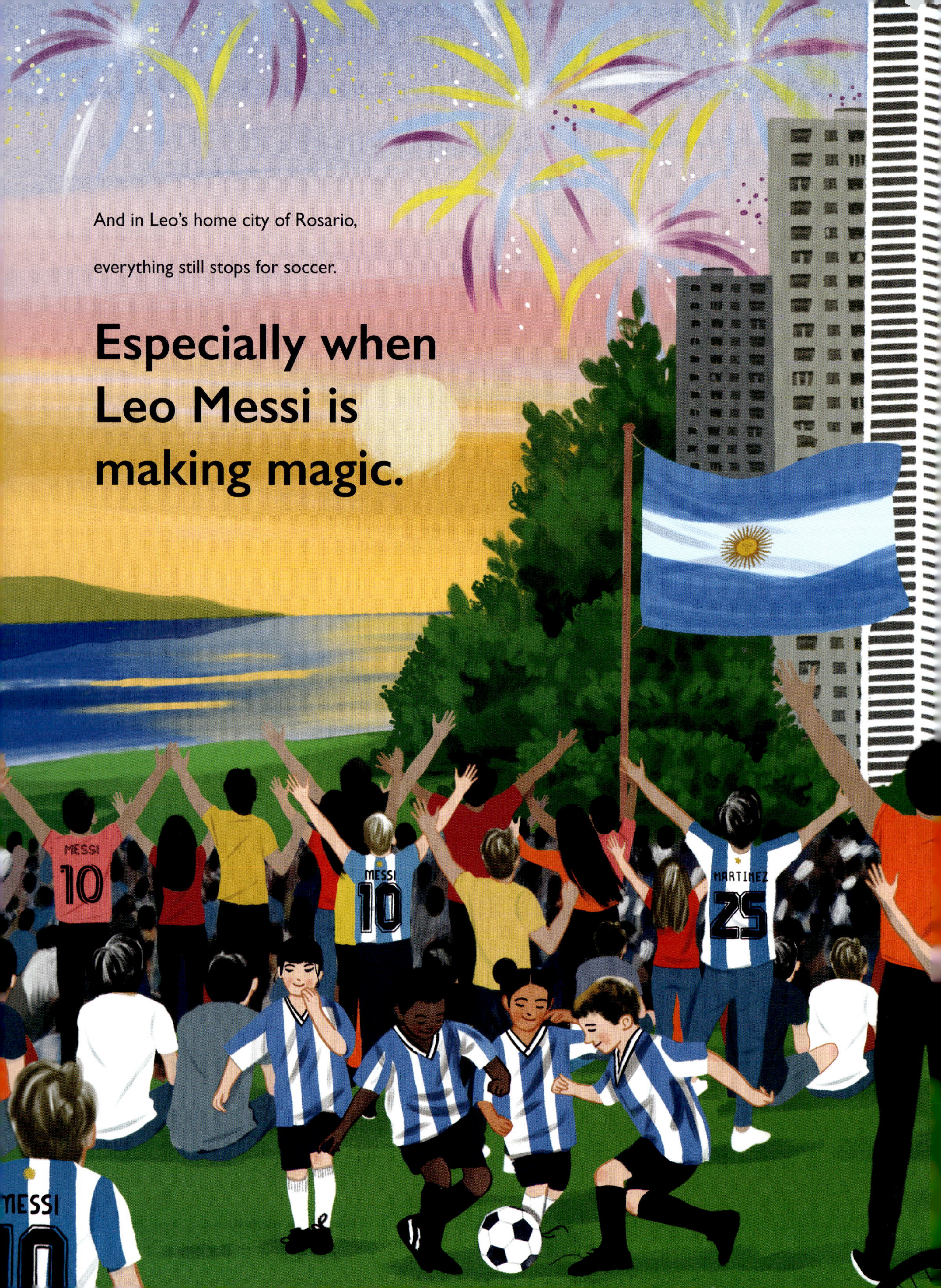

And in Leo's home city of Rosario,

everything still stops for soccer.

Especially when Leo Messi is making magic.

MESSI
10
MESSI
10
MESSI
10
unicef

June 24, 1987: Luis Lionel Andrés Messi Cuccittini is born in Rosario, Argentina, to mom, Celia María, who works in a facility that makes magnets, and steelworker dad, Jorge. He is called Lionel, or Leo, by his friends and family. Leo has two older brothers, Rodrigo and Matías, and a younger sister, María Sol.

1990: As a child, Leo plays soccer with his brothers and his cousins, Emanuel and Maximiliano Biancucchi, who also become professional soccer players.

1991: When Leo is four years old, he joins local club Grandoli, encouraged by his maternal grandma, Celia. His father, Jorge, becomes his coach.

1993: Six-year-old Leo starts playing for Rosario's Newell's Old Boys club. His team loses only one game in four years, and they become known as "The Machine of '87." Here, shy Leo makes lifelong friends.

1998: Leo's grandma Celia dies.

1999: Doctors diagnose Leo with a growth hormone disorder. Without expensive treatment, he won't grow anymore, and he won't be able to play professional soccer.

2000: Argentina is in the grip of a financial crisis, and Leo's parents can no longer afford to pay for his medical treatments. Leo is invited for a trial at FC Barcelona. Within minutes of seeing Leo play, Charly Rexach, FC Barcelona's sporting director, decides to sign the young player, but club rules make it complicated to sign foreign players at such a young age. After three months of waiting, Leo's dad says that if his son doesn't see commitment from the club, he will take him back to Argentina. Rexach doesn't want to lose the wonderkid — he draws up a contract on the back of a napkin!

2001: Leo and his family move to Barcelona, and Leo enrolls in Barca's youth academy, La Masia. Leo struggles with loneliness when his mother and siblings return to Rosario.

2001–2004: In Barca's youth academy, Leo shines. His former La Masia training mate Gerard Piqué remembers: "He's the only player that I can recall seeing play for the first time, way back when we were thirteen years old, and saying to myself: 'Oh, this kid comes from somewhere else. This is not human. He is an assassin. He's the greatest I've ever seen.'"

2003: Aged just sixteen, Leo is brought on as a seventy-fifth-minute substitute for FC Barcelona's first team in a friendly game against Porto.

UT MESSI! MORE ABOUT MESSI!

2004: Seventeen-year-old Leo makes his competitive team debut in a game against Espanyol.

2005: Leo plays his first game with the Argentina national team, but his international debut ends in disaster. Immediately after joining as a substitute against Hungary, Leo swings his arm in an attempt to wriggle free from a marker who is tugging his shirt. Leo is given a red card and sent off after less than one minute!

2006: Leo makes his World Cup debut for Argentina when he is just eighteen years old — the youngest ever Argentine player in the tournament.

2008: Leo plays with Argentina in the Olympics. His team wins the gold medal.

2009: FC Barcelona wins the UEFA Champions League, helped by a glorious Messi goal.

2013: A golden replica of Leo's legendary left foot is auctioned off for a cool $5,000,000, raising money for Messi's children's charity, the Leo Messi Foundation.

2014: Argentina loses to Germany in the World Cup finals.

2014–2022: Leo wins dozens of trophies and smashes goal-scoring records.

2016: Argentina loses the Copa América final to Chile. Leo misses his penalty and announces his retirement from international soccer. "I've tried my hardest and it isn't to be," he says, thinking he'd let his country down. The next day, Argentine newspapers run campaigns asking him to change his mind. Everyone wants him to keep playing! A few weeks after retiring, Leo reverses his decision.

2022: Leo helps his national team to lift the World Cup trophy after a triumph against France. Before the final penalty goes in, an emotional Leo appears to look up to the skies and speak to his late grandmother, saying, "Puede ser hoy" ("It could be today"). Later that year, Leo moves from Barcelona to join French team Paris Saint-Germain.

2023: Leo announces a move to MLS team Inter Miami, bringing Messi Mania to the United States! He is named *Time* magazine's Athlete of the Year.

2024: Inter Miami captain Leo is named the Landon Donovan MLS Most Valuable Player.

MESSI'S TROPHY CABINET

Leo is the most decorated soccer player of all time, with forty-four professional awards, including eight Ballon d'Or trophies, the most for any soccer player, and a record six European Golden Shoes. With FC Barcelona, Leo won thirty-five major trophies, making him the most successful player in the club's history. Leo also holds the record for most goals scored in Spain's La Liga (474), most hat tricks in La Liga (36), most assists in La Liga (192), most goals in the Supercopa de España (14), and most hat tricks in the UEFA Champions League (8). He has the most recorded assists in professional soccer history (374 and counting at the time of this publication). Leo has scored more than 820 goals for club and country over the course of his professional career, and he is currently Argentina's highest-ever World Cup goal scorer. He helped Inter Miami clinch the 2023 Leagues Cup, the MLS team's first official trophy. In January 2025, Leo was awarded the Presidential Medal of Freedom, the United States' highest civilian honor, by President Joe Biden.

MORE MESSI FACTS

- Leo has never let his smaller stature get in the way of his dreams. Even as a child, his lightning-fast reactions, perfect positioning, and finishing finesse made him stand out from the crowd.
- Leo is predominantly a left-footed player.
- While at FC Barcelona, Leo worked with a nutritionist to improve his diet. He cut back on unhealthy foods (and chocolate cookies), and now he makes sure to eat balanced meals with plenty of fresh fruit and vegetables.
- Off the field, Leo is known for his charity work. He has established the Leo Messi Foundation, which improves the lives of vulnerable and disadvantaged children around the world. The foundation donated funds to restore a children's hospital in Rosario, Argentina, and helped establish a pediatric cancer center at Barcelona's Sant Joan de Déu hospital. Programs pay for pediatric doctors' medical training and free school breakfasts for schoolchildren in rural locations. The charity promotes access to health, education, and sports for all kids.
- Leo also works as a UNICEF Goodwill Ambassador. "Being a bit famous now gives me the opportunity to help people who really need it, especially children," he has said.
- Leo is still close with his family. His dad, Jorge, works as his agent, and his older brother Rodrigo manages his publicity and schedule. His mom, Celia María Cuccittini, manages the Leo Messi Foundation, while his sister, María Sol, is in charge of Leo's clothing line.
- Leo is married to his childhood sweetheart, Antonela Roccuzzo, and the couple has three sons, Thiago, Mateo, and Ciro, all budding soccer fanatics!
- Despite all his hard work and thousands of hours of practice, Leo still enjoys every moment on the field. "I have fun like a child in the street," he said. "When the day comes when I'm not enjoying it, I will leave football [soccer]."
- Leo currently plays for Major League Soccer team Inter Miami, which is partly owned by British soccer legend David Beckham. Since Leo's arrival in the United States, his team has broken MLS attendance records, with his presence filling stadiums and raising awareness of "the beautiful game." Leo's striking pink number 10 jersey is the bestselling jersey in America. Messi Mania is here to stay!

AUTHOR'S NOTE

Growing up in England, I was surrounded by soccer: It was a part of life, as comforting and constant as crumpets, scones, and mugs of steaming-hot tea. When the national team lost a game in a major tournament, a dense fog of disappointment would blanket the nation. But when they won, jubilation erupted, spilling into streets, stores, and school playgrounds across the country. Football (as we call it) was a rare, unifying force.

I first watched Messi play when he was a wonderkid at FC Barcelona, and it was hard not to be wowed: His style of play seemed almost otherworldly, a gift that graces the game perhaps once in a generation. As I learned more about his journey and the struggles he overcame to rise to the pinnacle of his sport, I realized that Messi is not only a phenomenal player but also a symbol of resilience and dedication. It's no surprise he's an icon to millions.

Now I live with my family in California, and I'm still surrounded by soccer. As a soccer mum and a volunteer youth soccer coach, I've also seen firsthand how "the beautiful game" can transform young lives. A once-shy kid blossoms into a star striker, and someone struggling at home or in school finds friendship and "family" within the inclusive embrace of a team. Together, every goal is celebrated, every loss is shared, and each player is essential.

Since Messi brought his magic to Inter Miami CF, it's been thrilling to watch a new generation of US soccer fans fall under his spell, with young devotees discovering a love for the sport in the process.

The G.O.A.T.'s legacy continues to grow, along with his legion of admirers. I hope Messi's story inspires and helps readers find the confidence to make their own magic, both on and off the field.

—C.P.

"When I retire, I want to be remembered as a good guy."

—Leo Messi

ARTIST'S NOTE

It was a thrill to be asked to illustrate Caroline's beautiful text, which I found so inspiring. Right away, I began researching. I learned so much about football (soccer) while creating the art for this book and can now almost call myself an expert. That's one of the things I love most about illustration — you learn a lot about different subjects. Something that was important to me as I created the sketches was capturing Messi's poses and physiognomy so he would be recognizable to his legion of fans. Messi and I share an adopted city. When I drew him arriving in beautiful Barcelona, where he trained and developed into a professional player, I felt a real kinship with him as I reflected on how the city I now call home has helped me find my life's path as an artist.

—L.L.

For my very own superstar, Leo. —C.P.

To Kirsten at Catbird. —L.L.

During the course of my research, I read many interviews with Messi himself and those who have played alongside or worked closely with him. I pored over statistics from sources like fbref.com, whoscored.com, and transfermarkt.com; consulted various books, websites, and documentaries; and attended The Messi Experience, an officially endorsed interactive exhibition, to gain further insight into the G.O.A.T.'s life and career. I was also fortunate to witness Leo in action, scoring a glorious goal that helped Inter Miami triumph over LA Galaxy. Being immersed in Messi Mania with a sell-out crowd of soccer fans was a truly unforgettable moment.

My thanks go to my brilliant editor, Tracy Mack, and to Luca Caioli, the renowned sports journalist and author of *Messi: The Inside Story of the Boy Who Became a Legend*, for his fact-checking support. —C.P.

Library of Congress Cataloging-in-Publication Number: 2024041679

ISBN 978-1-5461-4753-4

10 9 8 7 6 5 4 3 2 1 25 26 27 28 29

Printed in China 38
First edition, September 2025

The text type was set in Gill Sans Regular and Gill Sans SemiBold. • The display type was set in Messi Font. The illustrations were created in Procreate on an iPad Pro. • Production was overseen by Lisa Broderick. Manufacturing was supervised by Juliann Guerra. • The book was art directed and designed by Marijka Kostiw and edited by Tracy Mack.